NORTH AMERICAN NATURAL RESOURCES

TIMBER
AND FOREST PRODUCTS

North American Natural Resources

Coal

Copper

Freshwater Resources

Gold and Silver

Iron

Marine Resources

Natural Gas

Oil

Renewable Energy

Salt

Timber and Forest Products

Uranium

NORTH AMERICAN NATURAL RESOURCES

TIMBER
AND FOREST PRODUCTS

Jane P. Gardner

MASON CREST

Mason Crest
450 Parkway Drive, Suite D
Broomall, PA 19008
www.masoncrest.com

MTM Publishing, Inc.
435 West 23rd Street, #8C
New York, NY 10011
www.mtmpublishing.com

President: Valerie Tomaselli
Vice President, Book Development: Hilary Poole
Designer: Annemarie Redmond
Illustrator: Richard Garratt
Copyeditor: Peter Jaskowiak
Editorial Assistant: Andrea St. Aubin

Series ISBN: 978-1-4222-3378-8
ISBN: 978-1-4222-3389-4
Ebook ISBN: 978-1-4222-8563-3

Library of Congress Cataloging-in-Publication Data
Gardner, Jane P.
  Timber and forest products / by Jane P. Gardner.
      pages cm. — (North American natural resources)
  Includes index.
  ISBN 978-1-4222-3389-4 (hardback) — ISBN 978-1-4222-3378-8 (series) — ISBN
978-1-4222-8563-3 (ebook)
  1. Timber—North America—Juvenile literature. 2. Forests and forestry—North
America—Juvenile literature. I. Title.
  SD435.G37 2015
  634.90973—dc23
                              2015005852

Printed and bound in the United States of America.

First printing
9 8 7 6 5 4 3 2 1

TABLE OF CONTENTS

Key Icons to Look for:

 Words to Understand: These words with their easy-to-understand definitions will increase the reader's understanding of the text, while building vocabulary skills.

 Sidebars: This boxed material within the main text allows readers to build knowledge, gain insights, explore possibilities, and broaden their perspectives by weaving together additional information to provide realistic and holistic perspectives.

 Research Projects: Readers are pointed toward areas of further inquiry connected to each chapter. Suggestions are provided for projects that encourage deeper research and analysis.

 Text-Dependent Questions: These questions send the reader back to the text for more careful attention to the evidence presented there.

 Series Glossary of Key Terms: This back-of-the-book glossary contains terminology used throughout this series. Words found here increase the reader's ability to read and comprehend higher-level books and articles in this field.

Note to Educator: As publishers, we feel it's our role to give young adults the tools they need to thrive in a global society. To encourage a more worldly perspective, this book contains both imperial and metric measurements as well as references to a wider global context. We hope to expose the readers to the most common conversions they will come across outside of North America.

Forest Regions of North America

N

	Taiga
	Northern Forest
	Temperate Forested Mountains
	West Coast Rainforest
	Eastern Temperate Forest
	Mediterranean California
	Tropical Dry Forest
	Tropical Rainforest

Note: Names of biomes can vary. For example, parts of Mediterranean California are sometimes called "subtropical dry forest." Similarly, some maps divide the temperate rainforest into "moist" and "wet."

Davis Strait

Hudson Bay

C A N A D A

UNITED STATES
OF AMERICA

ATLANTIC
OCEAN

PACIFIC
OCEAN

Gulf of Mexico

M E X I C O

Caribbean Sea

0 km	500	1,000
0 miles		500

0 km	500	1,000	1,500
0 miles		500	1,000

INTRODUCTION

When European settlers began to populate North America, the continent was covered in about a billion acres of forest. Today, roughly 750 million acres (3 million square km) remain as forest, or about 70 percent of the original area.

Those early forests of North America were diverse. Deciduous and coniferous forests were found in northern regions in both the East and the West, while pine forests covered the Southeast. Hardwoods, giant pines, and other conifers covered the mountainous regions of the United States and Canada. Mexico was home to forests of oak and pine, along with rainforests and dry forests. The northernmost regions

Temperate rainforest in Pacific Rim National Park, Vancouver Island, British Columbia. (Adam Jones/ Wikimedia)

of Canada consisted of boreal forests, also known as the taiga. These forests still exist, but they are much smaller than they were in the past.

With such diversity, the forests of North America provided an abundance of natural resources for the early settlers. They used the wood to heat their homes, cook their food, and build their houses. Later on, wood helped fire the steam engines and trains that traversed the continent. The forests were home to the birds, deer, and other animals that were a mainstay in the diets of the early people. Much of that has not changed today.

But what exactly is a forest? A forest is a large area densely populated by trees and the underbrush near the trees. Forests are very similar to what is commonly referred to as a *wood*. A wood, or the woods, is a smaller area that does not have as great a density of trees. The development, management, and cultivation of forest resources is a science called forestry.

This book explores the forests of North America. It also looks at the natural resources found there, not only the timber but the other resources as well. The forests of North America are known for their diversity and beauty, and they are a resource that needs to be protected for future generations.

Chapter One

FORESTS OF NORTH AMERICA

When you think of a forest, you probably imagine tall trees hovering over the cool ground that is covered in soft pine needles. Or maybe you envision a thick **underbrush** with dead logs and branches everywhere. Or perhaps a quiet pathway with gently falling colored leaves scattered around. The forest of North America can look like any of these.

Words to Understand

biodiversity: all the living things in an area, or on Earth as a whole.

conifer: a tree that stays green all year.

deciduous: to lose something at a certain point in development.

precipitation: water that falls from the clouds in the form of snow, sleet, hail, or rain.

taiga: an ecosystem found in the northernmost regions of Canada and Alaska; also called boreal forest.

underbrush: small shrubs and trees that make up the undergrowth in a forest.

Deciduous trees in autumn. Leaves are green because of a chemical called chlorophyll. As the leaves lose their chlorophyll, they change color.

Deciduous Forests

The trees in a **deciduous** forest lose their leaves each autumn. They pass the winter with no leaves, only to grow new ones in the spring. Elms, oaks, maples, and ash are all deciduous trees. In North America, deciduous forests are found in regions in the East—from Texas to Minnesota, and Florida to Maine—and in a small area in Canada around the Great Lakes.

A deciduous forest receives between 30 and 60 inches (76–152 centimeters) of **precipitation** each year. These forests have four unique and specific seasons each year: summer, fall, winter, and spring. As the seasons change, so do the trees.

Other types of plants are found in the deciduous forest. The soils on the forest floor are very rich and fertile, making it the perfect environment for small plants such as wildflowers, mosses, and lichens to grow. A layer of smaller trees and shrubs can be found in the forest as well, under the larger trees.

A deciduous forest is home to many different types of wildlife. White-tailed deer, black bears, turkeys, opossums, skunks, raccoons, and foxes all make a deciduous forest their home. Smaller mammals like squirrels and chipmunks share the forest floor with toads, frogs, and salamanders.

There are many natural resources found in a deciduous forest, and timber is by far the most important. Hardwoods like maple and oak are popular flooring options

Hardwoods and Softwoods

The term *hardwood* does not necessarily mean that a particular wood is harder than another. In fact, there are *soft hardwoods*, such as balsa, and *hard softwoods*, such as yew. The terms are used to describe the biology of the tree and the way that the wood is formed.

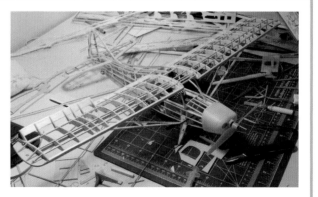

Model airplanes are often made from balsa wood. Even though balsa is called a hardwood, it is actually quite soft and lightweight.

and are also used in construction. But there are other resources, too. Hunters use the deciduous forests to hunt for deer and Thanksgiving turkeys. Trappers may use the forest to get deer, bear, or fox hides. People fish in the streams and lakes of a forest. They also use the forests for recreational pursuits such as hiking, cross-country skiing, and mountain biking. Resources such as pecans, walnuts, and mushrooms are found in these forests. And don't forget about maple syrup!

Coniferous Forests

Coniferous forests have trees with needle-shaped leaves. These trees, called **conifers**, hold their leaves all year long, keeping their green color even in the coldest winters (for this reason, they are sometimes called *evergreens*). Conifers carry and spread their seeds through cones. Pine trees, hemlocks, and spruce trees are all conifers.

Coniferous forests are home to a variety of mammals including moose.

Mixed Forests

Not all forests are made completely of either deciduous or coniferous trees. "Mixed forests," with some of both types of trees, are especially common in the eastern regions of the United States and Canada, as well as around the Great Lakes. These forests include trees such as oaks, beeches, maples, and birches, as well as pines, firs, and spruces.

The forest in Denali National Park, Alaska, contains both coniferous trees, such as pines, and deciduous trees, such as birches.

Conifers grow best where there are short summers and long winters. This is the case in the northern sections of North America and other continents. Some of these areas may have heavy snow for about half of the year.

These trees are perfectly adapted for their cold, snowy environment. The needles on the trees often have a coating that feels somewhat waxy; this helps prevent the loss of water. The branches are long and bend easily, which allows them to ride out the heavy snow that falls.

The floor of a conifer forest is different from that of other forests. When the needles of these trees die, they fall to the ground and pile up. The ground takes on a soft, almost spongy feel underfoot. The needles are rather acidic, which makes the soils of conifer forests less fertile than others. Conifer trees can grow to great heights and often block

Fire and Pines

Forest fires are not always something to be avoided. In fact, some trees in a coniferous forest depend on them. For example, jack pine has cones that are coated in a waxy substance. In order for the seeds to be released from the cone, the waxy coating has to melt. The heat of a forest fire is what makes that happen. The fire melts the coating, and the seeds are released and spread by the wind. Jack pines are usually the first to grow in the newly scorched forest. They are a *pioneer species*, meaning that they are among the first organisms that move into an ecosystem that has been disrupted or damaged.

the sunlight from reaching the forest floor. This means that there are generally not a lot of other plants or shrubs growing on the floor of a conifer forest. But shade-loving plants, such as ferns, mosses, lichens, and mushrooms, do thrive beneath the conifers.

Coniferous forests tend to be home to more mammals and insects than to amphibians and reptiles. These animals are better adapted to the longer winters. Moose, bighorn sheep, black bears, and bald eagles are found here. Owls, loons, and snakes often live in coniferous forests as well.

The northernmost regions of Canada are part of the **taiga**, an ecosystem characterized by harsh winters and short, humid summers. Some of the animals here hibernate during the rough snowy winter, some migrate to more southern climates, and some are adapted to the harsh conditions of this environment. There are many, many insects in the taiga during the summer months. The harsh conditions are not suitable for many plants, but the taiga is home to coniferous forests. Pines, spruce, and fir trees grow in tight clusters. This offers the trees some protection from the wind and extreme cold.

Rainforests

Believe it or not, there are rainforests in North America. They are found on the west coast of the United States and Canada. This includes places such as Olympia National Park, Mount Rainier National Park, Mount St. Helens National Volcanic Monument, and areas of British Columbia. These parks and regions have some of the biggest areas of old-growth rainforest trees anywhere.

Temperate rainforests receive 100 inches (254 centimeters) of precipitation a year or even more, and they have average temperatures between 39 and 54°F (4–12°C). There is a lot of fog in these forests. Another characteristic is that the trees cover nearly three-quarters of the sky when viewed from the forest floor. The **biodiversity**

The Hoh Rainforest in Olympia National Park receives between 140 and 170 inches (356 and 432 centimeters) of rain every year.

of trees in temperate rain forests is not large. There may be hundreds of different tree species in a tropical rainforest, but only 10 to 20 in a temperate rainforest. The trees here tend to have needle-shaped leaves and can live from 500 to 1,000 years! Temperate rainforests are located in coastal areas, where the moist air from the ocean meets high mountains and creates a lot of precipitation.

Mexican Dry Forests

Along the Pacific coast of Mexico, a rather unique ecosystem exists: tropical dry forests. These forests are similar to rainforests in that they receive a great deal of rain. However, a dry forest also has a long period of drought each year. These droughts can last for several months, which requires the organisms living there to face unique challenges.

Most of the trees in a dry forest, such as the ones in Mexico, are deciduous. They lose their leaves during the dry season. A tree loses much of its moisture through its

A pine–oak forest in Alvaro Obregon, Mexico, during the dry season.

leaves in a process called *transpiration*. Losing the leaves in the dry season allows the trees to survive and conserve water.

Dry forests are rich in biodiversity. There are not as many different species as there are in a tropical rainforest, but there are many species of plants, mammals, reptiles, insects, and birds. The dry forests of Mexico are home to rare bats, tarantulas, pumas, ocelots, jaguars, and many species of reptiles and amphibians.

The dry forests in Mexico are in danger. Tourism and the exploitation of wildlife are threatening the biodiversity of these forests. Ranches, the construction of roads, and farming are resulting in clearing much of the land. There are many efforts now underway to preserve and protect the Mexican forests.

Old-Growth Forests

An old-growth forest is a specific type of forest. It can have both old and young trees, as well as underbrush and wildlife. But a forest with old trees is not necessarily an old-growth forest. The exact criterion for calling a forest an old-growth forest is debated. Some say a forest can only be considered old-growth if there has been no human intervention. Others don't feel that this standard is necessary. Either way, old-growth forests have remained largely undisturbed for at least 100 years, and they are therefore unique environments.

Along the coasts of California, Washington, and Oregon, old-growth forests are home to some of the most well-known trees in the world—the giant redwoods. Redwoods (and their close relative, the sequoias) are conifers. Redwoods can grow to be about 30 feet (9 meters) in diameter and upwards of 250 feet (76 meters) tall. They can live for up to 3,000 years.

In the 1800s, more than 2 million acres of redwood forest covered the coast of California. Today that number is far, far smaller. As this area was settled in the mid-1800s, the clear-cutting of these forests was unchecked. Finally, in the 1920s, conservationists looked at these forests as a resource to preserve. The Save the Redwoods League helped set aside land as state parks to preserve these forests. Redwood National Park was established in 1968, and conservation efforts continue today.

The largest sequoia is a tree that has been named "General Sherman." This tree is found in Sequoia National Park in California. Its trunk is 102 feet (31 meters) in circumference, and it is 275 feet (84 meters) tall.

GENERAL SHERMAN

TEXT-DEPENDENT QUESTIONS

1. What are three ways that humans use deciduous forests? What other natural resources besides timber do people get from these forests?
2. Why are conifers sometimes called evergreen trees?
3. How does the biodiversity in a temperate rainforest differ from that of a tropical rainforest?

RESEARCH PROJECTS

1. Do you think old-growth forests should be harvested? Research both sides of the argument. Find out what scientific facts are used to support each stance.
2. Some redwoods can live to be 3,000 years old. Find out what major world events would have taken place in the time since such a tree began growing.

Chapter Two

FORESTRY PRODUCTS AND TECHNIQUES

Words to Understand

biodegradable: something that will decompose through natural processes.

cultivated: grown on a farm where the conditions are controlled.

decomposer: an organism that breaks down wastes and organic matter.

poaching: the illegal hunting or killing of animals or gathering of plant species.

sap: a fluid that moves through a plant; in maples and some other trees, it can be tapped and processed.

I f you look at a photograph of a forest, undoubtedly the first things you notice are the trees. Trees, primarily in their use as timber, are the primary natural resource we get from the forests. But, upon closer inspection, there are many other resources available. These resources, along with the available timber, must be carefully managed in order to most effectively use the resource now and in the future.

Maple Syrup

Mature maple trees, characterized by trunks that are at least 12 inches (30 centimeters) in diameter and a large canopy will produce the most sap. It is important to watch the temperature in late winter and very early spring to know when it is time to tap a maple tree. When daytime temperatures reach 40°F (4.4°C) or higher, and nighttime temperatures dip below freezing, then the sap within the structure of the tree begins to flow. In order to capture the sap running within the structure of the tree, a small hole is drilled into the tree. Then a small

A maple tree with a tap to collect sap, which will become syrup.

A Long Wait

It takes about 40 years for a maple tree to grow large enough to tap for maple syrup. After that, the tree can produce sap indefinitely. Some trees that are being tapped now have been around since the US Civil War in the 1860s.

A sugar maple tree in Whonnock, British Columbia.

tap is placed into the hole so that it reaches about 2 inches (5 centimeters) into the tree. There is a hook on the end of it from which a sap bucket, with a cover, can be hung. When conditions are right, the sap will flow in the bucket.

Sap is a thin, light-colored liquid. It is sweet, but not sweet like syrup. Maple syrup is made by boiling the water out of the sap. In general, it takes 40 gallons (151.4 liters) of sap to make 1 gallon (3.7 liters) of syrup. This helps explain why pure maple syrup is so expensive. Some of the most popular brands of syrup in stores are not made from maple sap at all; they are made of corn syrup and coloring, so they are less expensive than real maple syrup.

Christmas Trees: Real or Fake?

In recent years, people have become more thoughtful about the environmental impacts of the choices they make. For people who celebrate Christmas, this inspires a tricky question: What is better for the Earth, a real Christmas tree or an artificial one?

Some people take issue with the idea of cutting down a live tree only to throw it away a few weeks later. Artificial trees, by contrast, are reusable. If you invest in one, you can use it again and again, rather than destroying a new tree every year. However, artificial trees are usually made from plastic, which is not especially environmentally friendly. You also have to consider the impact of the factory that made the tree in the first place. Many artificial trees are shipped from China, adding to their environmental impact. And it's not uncommon for artificial trees to end their lives in landfills, which contributes to the problem.

On the other hand, real trees are biodegradable. They can be recycled and turned into mulch or compost. It is also worth considering the fact that Christmas tree farms are a big business, employing some 100,000 people during the season and taking up about 350,000 acres of land in the United States. That's a lot of land devoted to trees that might otherwise be sold to developers.

In the end, experts say that both live and artificial trees have equal— and ultimately pretty minor— impacts on the environment. But if you are concerned about the impact of your seasonal decorations, the American Christmas Tree Association makes the following recommendations: (1) if you choose a live tree, buy one that was grown locally if possible, (2) consider how far your tree (whether artificial or real) had to travel to get to you, (3) reuse artificial trees for a minimum of 9 years, and (4) be sure to properly dispose of your real tree.

Edible Mushrooms

Mushrooms are an important part of many recipes and foods. Most likely, the mushrooms in your local supermarket or in a salad bar were grown on a mushroom farm. However, many mushrooms are found in the forests of North America. Mushrooms can be harvested from the forest floor, or from the decaying logs found there. But they can also be **cultivated** as a business. In fact, it is possible not only to harvest, but also to farm, exotic mushrooms in the forest. Mushrooms such as shiitake, maitake, and oyster mushrooms can also be grown in a forest, generally by a farmer who specializes in using forest resources to grow crops.

Mushrooms grow best on the logs of hardwood trees. Mushroom farmers cut down hardwood trees as part of their regular forest management. The logs are cut during the winter and early spring. Special care is taken while cutting the trees to make sure that the outer layer of bark is not damaged. A series of holes are drilled into

A pink oyster mushroom growing on an oyster farm.

Don't Eat That

Not all mushrooms are edible. In fact, some are very poisonous! If you head out to the forest and see mushrooms, be careful. Never eat a mushroom unless you are sure you can identify it. Take a class, consult guidebooks, or ask an expert. If you aren't sure if a mushroom is safe to eat—don't eat it!

Calocybe carnea is an edible mushroom that is common to North America, but it looks very similar to certain poisonous mushrooms.

the logs, and mushroom spores are injected into the holes. The logs are then arranged to make sure that the mushroom spores get the right amount of moisture and air circulation and that the temperature stays ideal for mushroom growth.

About 6 months later, with careful watering and attention, the mushrooms will be ready to harvest. Mushrooms can be picked daily, and the logs may produce them for a long time. A family might set up a system of 10 logs or so for their own personal use, while a small commercial operation may have 500 logs. In larger commercial operations, mushrooms can be produced on thousands of logs.

Ginseng

Among all the plants that populate the forest floor, there may be some that can be turned into medicine. One of the most common and most talked-about herbal medicines is ginseng. Some believe that this root has been shown to increase the immune system, reduce the effects of a cold, increase concentration, and manage blood sugar. So far, there is no scientific evidence supporting all of these uses. But this hasn't stopped people from buying ginseng and ginseng products.

Ginseng grows in the hardwood forests in the eastern United States and southeastern Canada. Ginseng is sensitive to heat. Consequently, in the South, it is found in the mountains, such as the Appalachians. It will usually be found in shady areas, behind rocks or large trees.

Fresh ginseng root.

It is illegal to harvest wild ginseng in many places. Be sure to check with the local and state regulations before gathering ginseng.

Ginseng is an important player in the health and productivity of a forest. Fungi

A Costly Herb

In 2011, three men were given fines and jail time for poaching ginseng from Great Smoky Mountains National Park in North Carolina. The men were found with over 11 pounds (5 kilograms) of ginseng, which they gathered in one day. One man was fined $5,540 and ordered to serve 75 days in jail, while the others received lighter sentences.

and other **decomposers** are found on the forest floor. Decomposers break down the chemicals from dead organisms and waste products and return them to the soil. This recycles the nutrients in the ecosystem. Ginseng provides nutrients for the decomposers. As a result, the practice of **poaching** ginseng has become of great concern to environmentalists, foresters, and others. While the poaching of elephants for their ivory tusks gets a lot of attention, the poaching of a small root is not as exciting. However, poachers know the risks and still gather the herb illegally. In some markets, a pound of wild ginseng can be worth $800!

Animals

Hunting, trapping, and fishing are activities that utilize nontimber forest resources in a forest.

Hunters obtain permits to hunt game animals, such as white-tailed deer, pheasant, quail, turkey, duck, geese, black bear, and rabbit. Hunting licenses are acquired through state and local offices. In some cases, there is a limit to how many of an

A white-tailed fawn in the Pennsylvania woods.

The opossum is the only marsupial in North America.

animal a person may kill on a given hunt, and a maximum number that one hunter may kill each year. This helps control the population of the animal and also helps to manage the other natural resources in the forest. Most game is hunted only during a particular season, to ensure the cycle of life is not disrupted and the population of the animal is not too greatly affected.

Other, smaller animals can be trapped for their fur, such as raccoons, foxes, weasels, and opossums. Others are trapped for perfume. Believe it or not, a certain part of a wild beaver, called a castor, is used to make perfume. Animals are also trapped if they are considered to be pests. Foxes, beavers, bobcats, and raccoons can all do damage to crops, households, livestock, and property. One way to control those pests is to trap the animals. Those wishing to trap animals, for any reason, need to secure the proper permits and licenses from their state or local government.

Forests are home to some of the most beautiful and biologically rich bodies of water. Lakes, streams, ponds, and rivers all dot the forests of North America. Those wishing to fish in these waters must obtain a fishing license from their state or local government. (For more on water resources, see *Marine Resources* and *Freshwater Resources*, two of the volumes in this set.)

TEXT-DEPENDENT QUESTIONS

1. Maple syrup is made from sap. How is the sap gathered and processed?
2. Some forest animals are trapped. What reasons are there for an animal to be trapped? Which animals are trapped?
3. Why is gathering ginseng illegal in some areas? What role does ginseng play in a forest ecosystem?

RESEARCH PROJECTS

1. What are the requirements to get fishing or trapping license in your state? How do you go about doing that? What animals or fish might you be able to catch in your area?
2. Can you identify common mushrooms? Take a guidebook with you to the supermarket and see if you can identify the ones in the vegetable aisle. What characteristics do these varieties have?

Chapter Three

USING TIMBER

Words to Understand

pulp: the material made by using chemicals to separate the fibers in wood.

sapling: a young tree; one with a trunk that is less than 4 inches (10.16 centimeters) in diameter.

seasoning: the process of drying lumber for use; sometimes done in kilns.

There are five basic steps that need to be taken to prepare timber for commercial use.

The first step is cutting down or *felling* the trees. In a forest, mature trees are often picked ahead of time to be harvested initially. This will leave the younger trees behind to grow. New trees, or **saplings**, will grow in the new spaces created.

The trees that are picked for cutting are usually felled in the winter. This is when the trees contain the least moisture, making them lighter to transport. The number of trees to be cut determines the tools that are needed. If a few are slated to be cut in a day, a chainsaw may be enough to tackle the job. More trees may call for larger teams of tree cutters and more heavy-duty machinery.

To cut down a tree, all it takes are four cuts with a chainsaw. Two cuts are made in one side of the tree, carving out a V-shaped hole. Another V-shaped cut is made in the other side of the tree. The logger is thus making two triangles in the tree, so that it is balanced as if on a hinge before the last and final cut. This helps the logger control where and when the tree falls. Right before the final cut, the logger may shout out "Timber!" to alert others that the tree is coming down.

Once the tree is on the ground, the limbs are cut from it, and the big tree is cut into smaller, more manageable logs. The logs are then stacked until it is time to ship them to the sawmill. This stacking does more than keep the lumber in easily accessible piles. It also provides time for more moisture in the logs to evaporate. Many trees may be more than 50 percent water, so allowing time for as much water to evaporate as possible will lighten the load significantly.

This photo shows the V-shaped cut made to fell a tree.

Safety First

Lumberjacks make a V-shaped cut in a tree to help direct where it will fall. There is no guarantee that things will go as planned, however, so they always have two escape routes planned, in case the tree begins to fall in an unintended direction. Care is taken before beginning to cut the tree to remove all the small trees and brush from the escape paths. Other people in the area are advised to stand far away from the tree—as far as 1.5 times the height of the tree.

The next step is to sort the logs. Logs of lower quality—smaller logs, or ones with many knots and imperfections in the grain—may be sent to a **pulp** or paper mill, where they are processed into paper. Other logs are transported to a sawmill, where they will be made into lumber.

Paper Mills and Sawmills

Once the logs are at the mill, the real work can begin. The logs are first passed through a machine that removes the bark. This machine is like a large, rotating drum. Several logs are placed in the machine at a time, so that they spin and hit each other, removing the bark in the process. Bark is not used in lumber or paper—instead it is used as fuel or in mulch.

At a paper mill, the logs are passed through a chipper. Here the log is reduced to pieces about 2 inches (5 centimeters) square. The chips are mixed with chemicals and heated. The resulting pulp is washed and bleached and pressed into mats. Further processing of those mats of pulp eventually creates paper.

Once the pulp is made, it is passed into a machine to make the paper. The pulp is sprayed into a thin layer on a moving wire screen. The screen is huge: it can be nearly 20 feet (6 meters) wide and moves at speeds of 60 miles (96.5 kilometers) per hour. The water in the pulp drips off while it is on the moving screen, leaving behind a matted sheet of damp cellulose fibers. This is then passed over rollers, which press it and dry it.

Logs destined for lumber are sent to the sawmill. Several different saws are at work at a sawmill. A head rig saw is one of the saws. This one makes a rough cut of a log. This helps ready the log for the different types of lumber it can become. The center-most part of a log is oldest and may have more knots than other parts. This wood is typically processed into heavy planks. The wood surrounding the center is younger and less knotty. It may become the lumber found in a home improvement store.

A tree becomes lumber at a sawmill.

The rough-cut pieces are then passed through a machine called an *edger*, which removes the rough edges. Lastly, the pieces are passed through a trimmer, which cuts the lumber into standard lengths. This whole process of cutting and forming the logs into boards is called *conversion*.

The final step is the **seasoning** of the lumber. There is still moisture in the wood at this point, even after all the steps it has gone through. The goal for most lumber is to get the moisture content to about 15–20 percent. Wood that has not been seasoned is referred to as *green*. Green lumber is more apt to twist and warp over time than seasoned wood. Wood may be seasoned naturally, by allowing it to dry at the sawmill. Usually, however, it is dried in a kiln.

After this process is complete, and the lumber has been properly seasoned, it is shipped to commercial outlets. Lumberyards, home improvement stores, hardware stores, carpenters, and the average homeowner now have access to the lumber from the forest.

The Deadliest Job

According to the US Bureau of Labor Statistics, in 2013, people working in the logging industry suffered the highest rate of fatal work injuries. Fatal injuries include accidents with equipment such as chainsaws and large machinery, as well as those caused by falling trees and tree limbs. The rate of fatal injury was over 91 per 100,000 full-time equivalent workers. That is one dangerous occupation.

TEXT-DEPENDENT QUESTIONS

1. How do loggers choose which trees to cut first?
2. Why are logs stacked after they are cut?
3. What are the uses of the bark from the trees?

RESEARCH PROJECTS

1. Find out more about how technology has advanced the job of loggers in the past 100 years. How has the equipment used to cut and process lumber changed?
2. Find out what it is like inside a sawmill. What tools, safety equipment, and products are found there?

Chapter Four

FOREST MANAGEMENT

Words to Understand

erosion: when soil or rocks are worn away by water, wind, or ice.

nonrenewable resources: natural resources that are not replenished over time; these exist in fixed, limited supplies.

renewable resources: natural resources that are replenished naturally over time.

sustainable: able to be kept at current levels.

s timber a **sustainable** resource? Is it **renewable** or **nonrenewable**? These are very important questions facing the timber industry today. When dealing with forested land, foresters and landowners alike need to decide how the resource will be managed. Some may opt to simply harvest the forest for immediate use. Others may formulate a plan to preserve and manage the natural resources in the forest.

The science of sustainable forest management is called *silviculture*. *Silvi* comes from the Latin term for forest. Picking the sustainable approach can help foresters and landowners manage the resources in the forest, which can provide income for years to come, protect the ecosystems in the forest, and maintain a habitat for plant and animal life for the future.

Clear-Cutting—Not Always So Clear-Cut

The term *clear-cutting* is somewhat unclear. Often the term is confused with *deforestation*, and two terms are sometimes used interchangeably. For this reason, clear-cutting is at times assumed to be completely negative. But, in fact, clear-cutting is a viable tactic used by silviculturists to harvesting timber from a forest. (Deforestation, which will be discussed later, is another issue.)

In the 1800s and early 1900s, clear-cutting in North America was the practice of cutting down all the trees in an area that could be used in a sawmill. This was typically the larger, old-growth timber. Clear-cutting at that time was done for economic

Clear-cutting in the Great Lakes region, circa 1965.

Seed Trees

Clear-cutting is not the only approach to forest management. One approach is called seed-tree cutting. For this approach, most of the trees in a given area are harvested, but between 2 and 10 trees per acre are left standing. The trees that are left behind are chosen for their genetics—they are tall, straight, and produce many seeds. The good seeds from these trees will fall on the fertile, cleared land and repopulate the forest. The forest will be thinner, with fewer trees that tend to be spaced out consistently. This approach is used for coniferous forests management more than with deciduous trees.

reasons. As a result of this practice, forests in the United States, Canada, and parts of Mexico were left in a fragile and ruined state.

The scientific discipline of forestry, and eventually silviculture, grew out of this experience. Scientists introduced an approach of selective cutting, where some trees were chosen for removal and others were left standing. This helped preserve the soils and also helped generate the growth of new trees.

In much of North America, the forests eventually grew back. But as the selective cutting techniques continued, loggers and foresters noticed a change in the forests. Selectively cutting the best timber left behind the smaller, less hearty trees. The overall quality of the timber became poor.

As a result, silviculturalists and foresters agreed that a new approach was necessary. The practice of cutting trees of similar age would allow the trees to take advantage of sunlight and soil resources while improving the quality of wood. This practice became known as clear-cutting—an unfortunate term, in the sense that it has gotten confused with the historical clear-cutting that was often done without regard for sustainability. This new clear-cutting practice refers to both the harvesting of the trees *and* the regeneration of the forest, with an eye toward improving biodiversity.

Deforestation

Deforestation is much different. Deforestation occurs when a forest, or large tract of forested land, is removed with no intention of replanting new trees or revitalizing the forest that once stood there. Deforestation is detrimental to the ecosystem, in part because it increases erosion. The lack of ground cover and roots directly exposed the soil to the elements.

Deforestation also has negative consequences for animal life, as the relatively sudden removal of their habitat has an irreversible impact on the species living there.

An aerial view of the border between Haiti and the Dominican Republic shows the effect of deforestation.

Trees play a vital role in the water cycle, returning water vapor to the atmosphere through the process of transpiration. Many deforested areas become almost desert-like over time. Trees and other plant species in a forest absorb carbon dioxide, a greenhouse gas, from the atmosphere. Cutting the trees not only reduces the amount of carbon dioxide that can be removed from the atmosphere, it also actually releases carbon dioxide. The trees hold carbon dioxide, and when they die, the gas is released. Overall, the impact that clear-cutting a forest has on the habitat, ecosystem, and climate can be significant.

Forest Fires

Watch the news during the summer months, and you're almost guaranteed to see a story about firefighters battling a massive forest fire, usually in the western parts of the United States. We are conditioned to expect that when there is a fire, it will be fought. Minimizing the damage done by fire is the goal of all firefighters everywhere, right?

Maybe not. When it comes to managing forest resources, sometimes a fire is a good thing. Suppose fires have been fought and stopped in a particular forest for years. The trees have built up and are now becoming stressed due to a lack of resources. A thick underbrush of shrubs and smaller plants crowd the forest floor, blocking sunlight from smaller species and using nutrients from the soil. Species of plants that depend on fire disappear. Dead and decaying logs and other material builds up in the forest. The next time lightning strikes a tall tree, that fuel lying around erupts into a massive forest fire—one that can't be easily controlled and could endanger not only the forest, but also the people in the area and the firefighters.

The approach of fighting every forest fire to the end is not necessarily the best for the forest. In the 1900s, the policy in the United States was to fight each and every forest fire so as to minimize the impact on the environment. It was in the 1960s that this policy began to be questioned, as people understood more about the role that fire plays in the health and growth of a forest. Today, wildfires and forest fires are controlled to the extent that they protect human life and property. But those factors aside, fires are often allowed to burn to help the ecosystem.

Forest fires are a chance for the forest to renew itself. Sometimes a forest service may set a fire on purpose. These fires are carefully planned, controlled, and monitored, by both firefighters and the forest managers. These fires can have a very positive impact on the forest. They can remove fuel that has built up on the forest floor; add nutrients to the soil; thin the forest, allowing for new growth; and remove nonnative species.

Other times, firefighters will allow a natural wildfire to burn to improve the health of a forest. They will closely monitor the flames and control the path of the fire for the maximum benefit to the forest.

Fire in a forest of ponderosa pine trees.

Pests and Diseases

It may be a strange way to think about it, but pests and diseases are a natural part of the forest ecosystem. A forest without any pests or diseases would be unhealthy. Pests and diseases that are native to the ecosystem can keep the food webs and cycling of nutrients within the forest in balance. For example, dwarf mistletoes are parasitic plants that affect the seed production of conifers in Mexican forests. But these plants are native to the ecosystem and are part of the natural balance in those forests.

It is the nonnative pests and diseases that typically cause the most damage within a forest ecosystem. Nonnative, or invasive, species are those that are not typically found in a particular ecosystem. Instead, they have been introduced, either accidentally or on purpose, into the area. Species that are native to the forest can be adversely affected by introduced species, though it can be difficult to predict how a forest ecosystem will react to such a threat.

In the 1940s, for example, a fungus known as Dutch elm disease was introduced into Canada. The fungus causes the leaves of the American elm tree to die, and this eventually kills the tree. This disease significantly, and dramatically, reduced the populations of elm trees in Canada and the United States.

The gypsy moth is not native to North America. It was accidentally introduced to the United States in 1869 by a man named E. Leopold Trouvelot. Trouvelot was an artist who also had a fascination with insects. He traveled to France and brought home gypsy moth eggs. Some moths escaped and began to live in the trees in his Massachusetts backyard. Trovelot knew what the insects could do and alerted local experts. They did not heed his warnings. Eventually, the infestation spread, and attempts to control the moth were unsuccessful.

The caterpillars of the gypsy moth eat the leaves of hardwood trees. This does not kill the tree, but it does impact the ultimate growth of the tree. Of particular concern is the impact that these pests have on oak trees.

A Healthy Forest

What is a healthy forest? It is a place where all of the parts, the good and the bad, the beneficial and the harmful, interact in a way that is ultimately good for the forest. This means that not all diseases and pests and fires and harvesting are to be avoided. Instead, they are managed to the ultimate benefit for all species in the ecosystem.

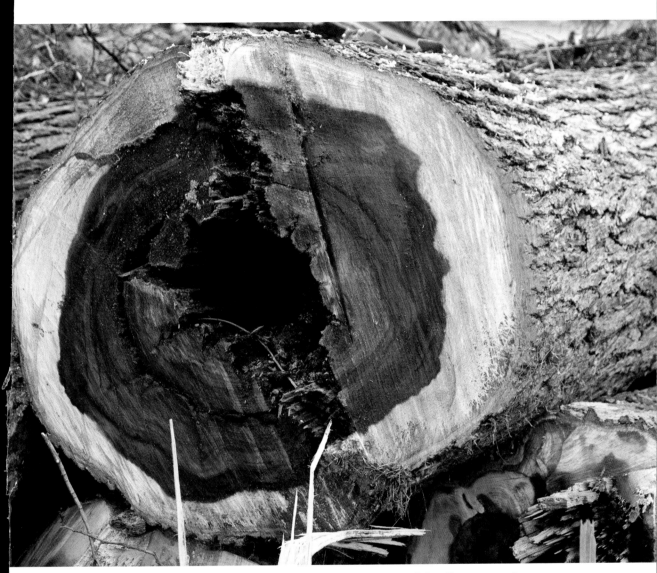

Trees with Dutch elm disease need to be cut down; the impact of the disease can be seen inside this tree.

There are steps that can be taken to prevent, or at least minimize, the damage done by these nonnative pests. The best defense would be to prevent the introduction of these species into the area. This is not always possible, so having a monitoring and detection plan in place is essential. Early detection of a nonnative species can lead to a rapid response to eliminate or control the potential pest.

Henry David Thoreau

Henry David Thoreau was an essayist, naturalist, poet, and activist who lived in the 1800s. He is well known for his collection of essays called *Walden; or, Life in the Woods.* In these essays, he wrote about the benefits of living a natural life, close to nature. He described feeling grief when a tree was cut down. He said of those who did not fully appreciate nature, "I would that our farmers when they cut down a forest felt some of that awe which the old Romans did when they came to thin, or let in the light to, a consecrated grove." Thoreau's works have been an inspiration to countless environmentalists, writers, conservationists, and nature lovers.

A replica of the cabin where Henry David Thoreau wrote his most famous work, in Walden Woods, Massachusetts.

Aerial view of a forest near Snow Shoe, Pennsylvania. The brown spots are trees whose leaves have been completely consumed by gypsy moths.

Early detection is successful when many people (land owners, farmers, hikers, and others) know how to identify the invasive species and alert the proper authorities. Educational programs and literature about these species is a vital first step to controlling a potentially devastating problem.

Once an invasive species has been identified, a combination of approaches to prevent and control the spread of the intruder is most effective. The species may be physically removed from the site. Pesticides or insecticides may be used. Reintroducing native species into the area can be effective as well. Another approach is to use biological controls. This means that natural predators are introduced into the area to control the nonnative species. This overall approach of using different methods to control and manage a pest is called an *integrated pest management* (IPM) plan.

TEXT-DEPENDENT QUESTIONS

1. What is the difference between historical clear-cutting and modern clear-cutting?
2. How can fighting every forest fire be bad for the forest ecosystem?
3. What is an integrated pest management (IMP) plan? What steps are taken when using IMP?
4. What is the difference between a native and a nonnative species?

RESEARCH PROJECTS

1. Deforestation has an impact on the carbon balance between the atmosphere and the surface of Earth. Find out how clearing tropical rainforest has impacted Earth's climate.
2. What nonnative species of insects are found in your area? What impact could they have on the plants and trees? Find out where they came from and what is being done to control them.

Chapter Five

OUR FORESTS— PAST, PRESENT, AND FUTURE

t's hard to look at a forest today and picture how it has changed from its original state. Often the trees seem to be so big that we believe that they must have been there forever. It's also easy to believe that they will be there for many years to come. That is not always the case, however. The forests of North America have changed greatly since the time of the first European settlers. And they are still changing today.

Words to Understand

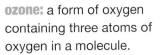

ozone: a form of oxygen containing three atoms of oxygen in a molecule.

paleobotanist: a scientist who studies the plant life of the past by indirect methods.

reclamation: restoring land to its former state.

Forests of the Past

Some of the best clues about what the forests of North America looked like hundreds of years ago come from descriptions written by early European settlers. This historical record sometimes provides clues about the conditions of the soils,

Early Writings

Not all of the early European explorers were specific about their observations of the forests in North America. For example, when Giovanni da Verrazano visited the coast of Maine in 1524, he noted, "nothing extraordinary except vast forests."

In 1796, another European who came to North America commented that "the most striking feature is an almost universal forest, starting at the Atlantic and thickening and enlarging to the heart of the country." He said that he "scarcely passed, for three miles together through a tract of unwooded or cleared land."

Mount Bigelow, West Peak, Maine.

the types of trees, and the height of trees. In particular, historians have found notes and letters discussing the availability of trees for shipbuilding. Early settlers were impressed by the expansive forests and the size of the trees themselves, since so many of the very big trees in Europe had been harvested long ago. Information from land surveys by early settlers also provides important insights into what our forests once looked like.

There are also other ways to look at the past. **Paleobotanists** and paleoecologists use fossils and other remains to infer what trees and plants once populated our forests. Pollen, insect, leaf, and cone remains preserved in bogs or ice help piece together some of the puzzles that remain. Boring cores in larger, older trees—which involves drilling a small hole in the tree and extracting a thin cylinder of wood—can help to determine their age, as well as the ages of the other trees in the area. Regardless of the specific trees in the forest, there is no doubt that the European settlers significantly changed the shape of the North American forests.

Forests in Transition

As the European settlers made North America their home, their impact on the forests was immediate. Forests in Europe had been depleted, making the business of shipbuilding difficult. Therefore, one of the first exports from North America was lumber. One year after their arrival on the Massachusetts coast, the Pilgrims sent their first shipment of lumber back to England aboard the ship *Fortune*.

The fuel, food, and lumber that the early settlers took from the forests helped them make North America their home. But most of the settlers were farmers and looked at the forests as an obstacle to their livelihood. With the aid of tools and animals and fires, the settlers cleared much of the forested land. This practice continued as North America became more settled and the westward migration of the citizens commenced. Estimates put the forested area in the United States in 1600 at about 1,200 million acres. By 1800, that area had dropped to just over 800 million acres, and by 1920, it was roughly 70 million acres.

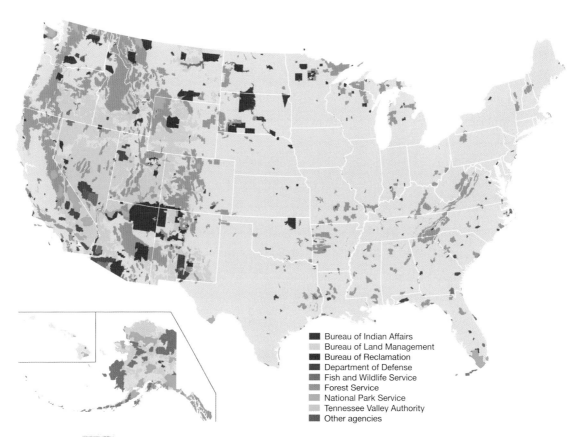

Bureau of Indian Affairs
Bureau of Land Management
Bureau of Reclamation
Department of Defense
Fish and Wildlife Service
Forest Service
National Park Service
Tennessee Valley Authority
Other agencies

This map shows the federally owned and managed land in the United States. The colors represent the federal bureau in charge of that land.

Forests Today

Many of the efforts to protect, preserve, manage, and conserve today's forests and natural resources were the result of the actions of President Theodore Roosevelt. Roosevelt was the 26th president of the United States, and he has come to be known as the "Conservationist President."

President Roosevelt took office in 1901. He formed the US Forest Service in 1905, and he appointed Gifford Pinchot as the first chief of this new agency. Pinchot described the mission of the agency as being "to provide the greatest amount of good for the greatest amount of people in the long run."

Roosevelt was president from 1901 to 1909. During that time, the forest reserves in the United States went from roughly 40 million acres to nearly 195 million acres. Today, the US Forest Service oversees 193 million acres of national forest and grasslands, and 36 million acres of wilderness area, national scenic areas, national monument areas, and volcanic monument areas. Roosevelt's vision is still in place.

The Conservationist President

Theodore Roosevelt was responsible for the creation of:
- 4 national game preserves
- 5 national parks
- 18 national monuments
- 24 **reclamation** projects
- 51 federal bird reservations
- 150 national forests

President Roosevelt on a hunting trip in Colorado, 1905.

The health and structure of our forests today are influenced by several factors. One is the demand for forest resources by humans. Forest resources such as timber for building and wood products for heating are needed at an increasing rate. Forested land is still cleared, although not at quite the rate it was in the past, to make room for new development and for livestock. Recycling efforts to reduce the need for wood for paper products have helped the situation. Reforestation efforts are working to replace timber and forest resources.

Mexico provides a good example. Conifers make up more than 80 percent of the Mexican timber industry. Policies are now in place to protect and renew these valuable resources. Most of the timber that is harvested comes from mountainous

National Park of Palenque, in Chiapas, Mexico.

regions that have few roads. Harvesting the timber has a significant impact on the environment and is very costly. Efforts to manage and conserve the resources in the Mexican forests have made a significant impact on the forests in these regions.

Today's forests are impacted by the need to suppress forest fires in many areas. Forest fires, as discussed in chapter four, play an important role in the overall health of a forest. Allowing some to burn naturally can be beneficial. But fires that can harm people or property need to be fought. Fighting fires to protect rural homes and the people who live there can impact the overall health of a forest.

Air pollution is also a factor in the health of our forests today. Studies have shown that acid rain and **ozone** in the lower atmosphere have the greatest immediate impact on the trees and plants in a forested area. Climate change is also impacting our forests today. But the greatest concern is the impact that climate change will have on forests in the future.

Forests of the Future

If climate change continues in the path that is anticipated, the impact on forests will be significant and varied. Climate change will certainly alter the growth of forests. Climate change is largely the result of increased carbon dioxide in the atmosphere. Carbon dioxide is needed for photosynthesis. This could mean that there forests will be more productive—more carbon dioxide means more photosynthesis, which means more growth. Predictions are that this will be true in areas with fertile soil and plenty of water. However, the increase in carbon dioxide will not have an impact on growth in areas with little water, such as the Southwest desert.

Another predicted result of climate change is an increase in the overall global temperature. At first, it might seem that an increase in temperature would extend the growing season for a forest. It could do this, but it could also impact the areas in which some trees will grow. This puts some trees and forests at risk. For example, if the trees that typically grow in the colder regions on top of mountains can't adapt to increasing temperatures at those altitudes, they will die off. Climate changes will result in more droughts in some areas, and more flooding in others.

Hurricane Danger

In 2005, Hurricane Rita and Hurricane Katrina destroyed or damaged nearly 5,500 acres of forest in the Gulf of Mexico region of the United States. That same year, Hurricane Stan hit Mexico, destroying 76 percent of the forest in Chiapas. The dead and decaying trees released as much carbon dioxide into the air as all the carbon dioxide taken in by all the forests in the United States in 1 year.

Hurricane Katrina making landfall on the Gulf Coast, as seen from space.

Climate change is also believed to affect the frequency and severity of natural events. Storms such as hurricanes, tornadoes, blizzards, and ice storms will most likely be more severe and possibly more frequent in the future if climate change continues. These events will impact the health of forests. Climate change will also increase the range and abundance of pests, diseases, and wildfires in certain areas.

TEXT-DEPENDENT QUESTIONS

1. What do writings from early settlers tell about the forests in North America?
2. Why was Theodore Roosevelt known as the "Conservationist President"?
3. What is the connection between forests and climate change?

RESEARCH PROJECTS

1. Find out more about the formation of the National Park Service. What changes has the agency been able to make in recent years?
2. What does a paleoecologist do? Research this career, including how one becomes a paleoecologist.

"To waste, to destroy, our natural resources, to skin and exhaust the land instead of using it so as to increase its usefulness, will result in undermining in the days of our children the very prosperity which we ought by right to hand down to them amplified and developed."

— Theodore Roosevelt
President of the United States (1901 to 1909)
Seventh Annual Message
December 3, 1907

Further Reading

BOOKS

Allaby, Michael. *Temperate Forests*. Ecosystem series. Rev. ed. New York: Facts on File, 2007.

Dauvergne, Peter, and Jane Lister. *Timber*. Cambridge, UK, and Malden, MA: Polity Press, 2011.

Kerr, Julie Casper. *Forests: More Than Just Trees*. New York: Chelsea House, 2007.

Kershner, Bruce, et al. *National Wildlife Federation Field Guide to Trees of North America*. New York: Sterling, 2008.

Nagle, Jeanne. *Coniferous Forests: An Evergreen World*. Biomes of the World. New York: Rosen, 2009.

Stenstrup, Allen. *Forests*. Greensboro, NC: Morgan Reynolds, 2009.

ONLINE

Bronaugh, Whit. "North American Forests in the Age of Nature." American Forests. http://www.americanforests.org/magazine/article/north-american-forests-in-the-age-of-nature/.

Natural Resources Canada. "Forests in Canada." http://www.nrcan.gc.ca/forests/canada/13161.

US Bureau of Labor Statistics. "National Census of Fatal Occupational Injuries in 2013." http://www.bls.gov/news.release/pdf/cfoi.pdf.

US Forest Service. "Urban and Community Forestry." http://www.fs.fed.us/ucf/.

US Forest Service International Programs. "Mexico." http://www.fs.fed.us/global/globe/l_amer/mexico.htm.

Series Glossary

alloy: mixture of two or more metals.

alluvial: relating to soil that is deposited by running water.

aquicludes: layers of rocks through which groundwater cannot flow.

aquifer: an underground water source.

archeologists: scientists who study ancient cultures by examining their material remains, such as buildings, tools, and other artifacts.

biodegradable: the process by which bacteria and organisms naturally break down a substance.

biodiversity: the variety of life; all the living things in an area, or on Earth on the whole.

by-product: a substance or material that is not the main desired product of a process but happens to be made along the way.

carbon: a pure chemical substance or element, symbol C, found in great amounts in living and once-living things.

catalyst: a substance that speeds up a chemical change or reaction that would otherwise happen slowly, if at all.

commodity: an item that is bought and sold.

compound: two or more elements chemically bound together.

constituent: ingredient; one of the parts of a whole.

contaminated: polluted with harmful substances.

convection: circular motion of a liquid or gas resulting from temperature differences.

corrosion: the slow destruction of metal by various chemical processes.

dredge: a machine that can remove material from under water.

emissions: substances given off by burning or similar chemical changes.

excavator: a machine, usually with one or more toothed wheels or buckets that digs material out of the ground.

flue gases: gases produced by burning and other processes that come out of flues, stacks, chimneys, and similar outlets.

forges: makes or shapes metal by heating it in furnaces or beating or hammering it.

fossil fuels: sources of fuel, such as oil and coal, that contain carbon and come from the decomposed remains of prehistoric plants and animals.

fracking: shorthand for hydraulic fracturing, a method of extracting gas and oil from rocks.

fusion: energy generated by joining two or more atoms.

geologists: scientists who study Earth's structure or that of another planet.

greenhouse gas: a gas that helps to trap and hold heat—much like the panes of glass in a greenhouse.

hydrocarbon: a substance containing only the pure chemical substances, or elements, carbon and hydrogen.

hydrologic cycle: events in which water vapor condenses and falls to the surface as rain, snow, or sleet, and then evaporates and returns to the atmosphere.

indigenous: growing or living naturally in a particular region or environment.

inorganic: compound of minerals rather than living material.

kerogens: a variety of substances formed when once-living things decayed and broke down, on the way to becoming natural gas or oil.

leachate: liquid containing wastes.

mineralogists: scientists who study minerals and how to classify, locate, and distinguish them.

nonrenewable resources: natural resources that are not replenished over time; these exist in fixed, limited supplies.

ore: naturally occurring mineral from which metal can be extracted.

ozone: a form of oxygen containing three atoms of oxygen in a molecule.

porous: allowing a liquid to seep or soak through small holes and channels.

primordial: existing at the beginning of time.

producer gas: a gas created ("produced") by industrial rather than natural means.

reclamation: returning something to its former state.

reducing agent: a substance that decreases another substance in a chemical reaction.

refine: to make something purer, or separate it into its various parts.

remote sensing: detecting and gathering information from a distance, for example, when satellites in space measure air and ground temperature below.

renewable: a substance that can be made, or a process used, again and again.

reserves: amounts in store, which can be used in the future.

runoff: water not absorbed by the soil that flows into lakes, streams, rivers, and oceans.

seismology: the study of waves, as vibrations or "shaking," that pass through the Earth's rocks, soils, and other structures.

sequestration: storing or taking something to keep it for a time.

shaft: a vertical passage that gives miners access to mine.

sluice: artificial water channel that is controlled by a value or gate.

slurry: a mixture of water and a solid that can't be dissolved.

smelting: the act of separating metal from rock by melting it at high temperatures

subsidence: the sinking down of land resulting from natural shifts or human activities.

sustainable: able to carry on for a very long time, at least the foreseeable future.

synthesis: making or producing something by adding substances together.

tailing: the waste product left over after ore has been extracted from rock.

tectonic: relating to the structure and movement of the earth's crust.

watercourse: a channel along which water flows, such as a brook, creek, or river.

Index

About the Author

Jane P. Gardner has worked in science education for nearly two decades. With master's degrees in geology and education, she taught science at the high school and undergraduate levels before becoming a science writer. Jane has written more than 20 nonfiction books for K–12 students and adults. Jane lives in Massachusetts with her husband and two sons.

Photo Credits

Cover

Clockwise from left: Dollar Photo Club/Kletr; Dollar Photo Club/Jaroslav Machacek; Dollar Photo Club/megasquib; iStock.com/val_th; Dollar Photo Club/alexthq13; Dollar Photo Club/Sherri Camp; Dollar Photo Club/josefpittner

Interior

Dollar Photo Club: 10 rob osman; 11 Serguei Liachenko; 12 steverts; 21 james_pintar; 26 eungchopan; 28 nicolaselowe.

iStock: 24 kwanchaichaiudom; 31 lovro77; 32 val_th; 33 prodrive2002; 34 JPStrickler; 41 ellend1022; 43 Multiart; 44 hlnicaise; 52 MorganLeFaye.

Library of Congress: 51 H.C. White Co.

NASA: 39; 54.

US Department of Agriculture: 37.

Wikimedia Commons: 13 Carol M. Highsmith; 15 Michael Gäbler; 16 Tropicoboreal; 18 Famartin; 22 Kyle Lawrence; 23 DR04; 25 Luridiformis; 27 David Baron; 45 Dhalusa; 48 petersent; 50 National Atlas.